CW01560446

Meditations
on a Dark Pattern

Ross Ion Coyle
2022

Meditation: 1

"I am a feature of the world. I am a part of the world. The world is a whole and I am a part. What abides at my very base is the very base of the world itself."

What is the nature of that base?

-It is generative and creative, it produces all from itself, yet it is empty of what is produced,

-it operates with free will and total understanding,

-it condenses will and understanding into physical forms, yet in doing so, limits them,

-it is thereby a self-limiting creative and understanding will, infusing it's creation, yet remaining in itself free.

-It being the source of change and time, it is in itself beyond space and time

-In manifesting as limited selves and the world, it lies at the root of 'ego' and dualistic experience.

-The ego and world are it's creative self-expressions, therefore all that exists as ego and world is contained within it unexpressed

-Ego, the appearance that is the world, and expression are all related to consciousness, therefore, it is through consciousness that it operates. What we call consciousness is intimate to its nature. It is a supra-consciousness.

Meditation: 2

The Great Absolute, Supreme Universal Consciousness, The One, has manifested this physical Universe of myriad transformations, forms, and dynamic patterns of nature, including this brief mortal body I find myself in.

The Supreme Mind, the Spirit, the Ultimate Self, the only real Person, is here within as my own self and the Self of all other selves. All that I see is a manifestation of the One, this self within is fixed upon That One.

This mortal self is but a single instantiation of the Eternal Self. From the perspective of this ordinary self, this Self is the 'no-self' beneath the mortal self, from the perspective of the ordinary consciousness, it is the great and all potent abyss of 'un-consciousness' from out of which the consciousness arises, into which it again dissolves.

Rest peacefully on the knowledge that all is the manifestation of the One Creative Consciousness, all the within, all the without. One, and One only.

Through the dynamic processes of this Earth, this One Self has embodied Themselves in multitudes of beings, yet remains a perfect and unblemished Unity. Everywhere, throughout the incalculable distances of the Universe, throughout the incalculable expanses of time, there is nothing apart from this One.

This One has been realised by the blessed and the wise throughout all the generations of human life on Earth, though through different names and in accordance with diverse natures and dispositions.

Realising that there is only One, be at peace –
Realise- One alone! And fear will dissolve

Meditation: 3

Brahman is all.
Wherever, whenever there is a sentience, there is atman.
Atman is brahman.

Discovered by the mystics of ancient India,
yet this Presence is the eternal.
Even in the dark forests of northern Europe, or the high Andean
dells, in the ages silent to us, humanity has had this door at the base
of its consciousness
leading to the absolute consciousness, the one Person.

Brahman is all,
Consciousness is atman
and atman is brahman

If consciousness is thought of merely as waking perception, then
yes, the Universe had a body before it developed eyes to open on
itself.

But consciousness is not merely waking perception
At the deep level consciousness and existence are one, mind and
matter are not two, being and non-being are aspects of a unity,
beyond but not excluding description:
God of myriad names

Meditation: 4

The entire life of the waking consciousness
is only the briefest shimmer
on the surface of an unfathomable deep.
Yet, it is on the surface that we must live
and meet the daylight,
knowing that we emerge from an infinite well
of existence, consciousness, bliss

We are only thoughts, momentary flashes
plays of light on a dark water
no real you nor I
One Self alone
One all-embracing Mind
And we are thoughts
born on the will
by this will sustained
into this will dissolving
One Mind, One Self, One Will
Whatever It gives rise to,
I should see as myself

Meditation :the Base

All of the aeons of the past universe, all the aeons of the future
All the vast expanses of space and the cycles of time
All the colours shapes and complexities we see, within and without
And all of those we see not
All of our stories, and hurts, and brief triumphs
All,
Arise from That,
which neither comes, nor goes,
does not become does not depart
Pure and all potent
Where no words or argumentation penetrate
Where all is resolved and returned
Real, Consciousness, One, and beyond number!
With that faith alone,
I can be I, and you be you,
and all things be all things
and be blessed

Meditation: 5

-The absolute means the unified totality of being, the source-foundation of all possibility.

-Since our consciousness is a part of it, we are intimately linked to it, yet can only appreciate it partially.

-It is a unity, since all interaction of limited things, either in harmony, or disharmony presupposes a common ground for interaction.

-It contains plurality as potentiality, presents plurality as actuality, since limitation engenders relative distinction between the limited things. We are limited things, bodies among other bodies, on the level of waking consciousness.

-It is full of itself, and still, though it presents as dynamic between its limited things.

-It is empty in itself of all relative things, so to the relative consciousness and it's discursive intellect, it appears as emptiness itself

-It is consciousness-like since the nature of consciousness is the unifying principle of diverse apparitions and actions, and that is what the waking world appears as. (*it is also a supra-consciousness since all limited consciousnesses are contained in it as potentiality*)

-it is creative since constructive limitation is a product of creativeness,

-it is the Presence that enfolds past and future presents.

-It is therefore beyond multiplicity, duality, duration. It is the opposite of relative, or limited being.

-It does not itself fail or succeed: it is pure self-sufficient existence. The eternal now, you could say.

-It is not itself movement, but it manifests as movement,

-not time, but manifests as time,

-not plurality, but manifests plurality.

-It is the all-encompassing ground on which all these limitations are located.

-Discursive thought comes with plurality, plurality comes through limitation. Conscious absorption in the Absolute is beyond discursive thought. The experience of enlightenment is said to be beyond words.

Meditation : the Unreal

So it is revealed of the Mother of the Universe.
'By the day that dawns, and the memory that wakes,
Know that this realm is unreal, though existent,
And the thoughts and worries that arise in thee,
based on this realm-
Verily, they are doubly unreal.
Real alone is She, the Consciousness, the Foundation
Real is She, thy true base, Matrix
Be free of anxieties, be mindful of the virtues
For mindful is She, caring, all powerful.
Though you realise not yet
I, the within, the without'

By 'this realm' is meant the waking, physical world. It exists, but it is in constant flux. It is unreal in that it is within time, whereas the consciousness is beyond time, though it extends into time, in mortal life. Mortal consciousness is the extension of consciousness into space and time. The arranging principle of space and time based on the consciousness. The consciousness is the Pattern. What is it that is ultimately conscious? It is that which is itself nothing of the world but at root of all in the world. It has all identities as its self-expressions. It is therefore the self of the nothingness before identity. It is a creative pattern before subject and object. Nishida Kitaro calls it an intuition. For Nishida, intuition is that principle which gives rise to the discursive thought in our own consciousness, that is the mysterious power beneath, at the base of conscious thought. That base of consciousness is the same base as that beneath the world of the myriad things. For Nishida, this mysterious principle, this unifying base and generative power is God.

Meditation: 6

Non-dualism
'Brahman and Sakti are not two,
Sakti and Maya are not two,
Jiva and Atman are not two,
Brahman is all,
Atman is Brahman'

'The One and it's Power are not two,
The Power and it's Manifestation are not two,
The limited self and the Supreme Self are not two,
The One is all,
The Supreme Self is One'

Meditation 7: Absence and Presence

'From Absence to Presence,
and again to again,
Time's tapestry weaving,
one pattern,
From One'

That which underlies the conscious self is the unconscious non-self. The latter precedes supports and reabsorbs the former. The former is the world of differentiation, of subject and object, of the many, of duration and extension, of 'this and that', it is the world of the seer and the seen, the artist and the artwork, the creator and the created. The latter is the undifferentiated, where subject and object are one, beyond duration and extension, where 'this and that' cease to be opposites, the realm preceding seer and seen, the creativity before creator and created, artistry as a principle before artist as person in relation to art.

It is the That, the ontological That which manifests as Presence, which remains unmanifest as Absence.

Poetry

Hail from the Half-Light
In my dark garden
Autumns imprint at twenty-one
Chill air, faint stars
Moon quickens the night earth
Resting on vastness,
breathing in the deep

Seems always November
Always November night
After '01
Just November night
There I half died
Hail from my half-light

No living morn
No December light
November again
Just November night.

In early darkness born,
Half died in half light
Quickening towards dusk
Into darkness dying,
into return

'Strong, unfolding all as Light'
Behold, the glory of God,
the Mother, the Consciousness of Brahman,
within the magnificence of creation
the Temple of the Universe
the eyes of the Beloved
the all encompassing,
within every mortal soul

Strong, unfolding all as Light,
Universal hinge
Casting forth all temporal things
The Hidden Ultimate
Source and pattern of the worlds

Where do I meet Her?
All the within, all the without.
Fully present is Her pattern,
Moon before Moonrise

From It, Time is suspended,
In Time, all things arise and dissolve,
Time, and light, and million millions,
Into Itself, the Dark Womb withdraws.

Towers of vision rise up,
of obsidian waters composed,
Repeating, repeating, perpetual thrusts
So bloom the worlds,
So they wilt, and return.

The Darkness Orison
From darkness to darkness,
Stitch by stitch,
Time's tapestry weaving
One Pattern,
From One

Great Rushing Vastness:
that is Becoming's World,
Sacred Dark and Mystery,
That is Deep divine.

Journeying towards the Sun's rising,
I found the Mother, in the form of mirror,
the setting Sun's horizon,
In mirror-form, there too.

From the Hall-porch of Night
It shines, becoming light and beings,
Consciousness, Unconsciousness,
Person, Pattern, Principle,
One, the Other, and All,

From stillness, change,
Yet on Stillness, it rests
unmanifest to manifest
yea, again to again,
should we see with mind's radiance
The unity of all

This Unity creates without desire,
This Unity loves without condition,
This Unity endures without dissolution,
That is the Heavenly Unity.

The Door of Night
Come, child of a knowing family,
Approach the Door of Night along
the flowered pathway of thy sleep
The Hosts of the Heavens slumber beyond
Come and behold them, and ask of the Dark
It's secrets.

The horned mantle crowns the porch
A door with stars studded
down purple blossomed stairs
Approach now, fearing nothing
though impotent demons appear,
brush calmly past and lordly
enter into Sentient Night

On the swift wings of dream,
I went down through the earth,
into the supreme vault,
of the Mind's eternal sky,
the cats of the six-team,
drew Her wagon on the air,
seated by the Mother,
we to Her twilit palace made haste,
and the lamps blazed on the runway,
mainlight, sidelight, then there,
up into Her keep, to learn the pattern's weave.

TAT

A great need-fire burning
In plays of light and change
On a single pivot turning
Bright heaven, dark to earth

Seeing all and nothing
Two gates, but just One Mind
to the busy intellect, emptiness,
fullness emptied of time.

Beyond the limitations
In freedom bound by naught
The world exists as many
One Mind alone is real

To Emptiness, as to Presence,
Twenty years of craving peace,
A great peace, and returning,
To Mother, Father
To One.

'From Absence to Presence,
and again to again,
Time's tapestry weaving,
one pattern,
From One'

Dream of the Woman

Where is the Woman,
With eyes like the Sun?
The pearl, purple nimbus
Window lit to morning

My life flies past me, away
like a dream between darkness and memory
Numbers rise, returning into dark
Deep earth dreaming
fast in the hill

What has all this been,
but fragments of a dream
Dreamed by a world
through a passing mortal form?

The world dreamed life,
Life dreamed a body,
The body dreamed a person,
The person dreamed and died,
The dream, then, returned
to the Substratum, as a memory,
To be brought to mind again
Rising, and falling anew

All this, the world, -
but the dream of the Substratum
Unending Pattern
Hem of the Great Queen

Visions of Elbe

Weeping by the hill, once arrived
Sad and joyful, yet,
Ioncu falls into sleep
Dreaming, he returns
before the living return
Resting by the foot of Elbe
As the last light beams
Glimmer on the grass

In the forest of giant trees,
on the high branches
As a man-wolf I lived
The glade-hidden book is near
Which the hunters below me seek
That book tells of the flame-haired lady
Drammu, whose high house of wood
was the fountain of spirits
Sorceress of worlds was She that is
Though Her spells move the stars,
Yet She remains unseen
A shadow by the upper side of the hill

I see the roads and the houses
by the river banks
The city, split through
with green tracks, far
The temple in the grave yard,
the mighty roofed school
The crags and the sand-isle
And the shark-haunted sea

Threnody One
'I was born of the early hours' dark,
I lived full until the edge of night
whereat, it was for me to behold
the nascent things, the patterns to unfold
In the next day beyond
the costly feted midnight
Early it was that I half-died,
in the morning
Through the awful hours
of sunlit excess unto collapse,
I passed in half-light, sorrow swaddled
Deathly have I been
throughout this heartbroken age
Living again I shall be
to witness these hours return.
May some rich slivers
of gathered wisdom remain
within my Deep to guide my thoughts
to greater beneficence
For the cycle next'

Threnody Two

He sits by the well of the Father
All alone, on the high Hill of Rain
Damp are the eyes,
of twenty years dimmed
Nettle wrapped bones,
in a forest of stone,
Memory's phantoms
chitter on the wind

'is it you I see on the bow of the clouds?
Friends that a century, from me, drew away?
days fly from me, like the streams to the well
thoughts fly towards rest,
on the pattern, to dwell
The tide coming in, warm waters swell

Lying down by the Grotto of Neiro,
In the shadow of the Throne of the Sun
Peace in raindrops,
clouds rolling out Death
Light patterns lie
darkling meadow, sounding sigh
And the deep roots greening
beneath failing breath

My life has flown from me,
as a wind in dream, near waking
Numbers pass, to numbers return
Rain, rain
Grotto and bones.

Avalanche
I have dreams of an avalanche
that regathers it's flow, repeating
On pure shores, in stillness
by the sea of time
A bridge that is crossed,
and yet not so.
Hillside of Heaven,
Throne and Holy Elbe

Elbe
Orange is the evening
Purple, the night
Half my life have I lived,
Half alive.
Navy, then green,
Then fawn is Holy Elbe
Silence in the house of dusk
Waiting peace in the middle sun
Star steps in the dimlit street
Glory-O
Rising in the red sky room
Maroon in the morning room
Radiant and ever returning is Elbe.

All beings seeking bliss,
From bliss they are born
By bliss sustained
Wandering aeons towards bliss
Into bliss are they resolved

Dargo, aye,
Dargo is all,
and Mamlo is Dargo

Blessing for a Youth
May the Great One bless thee with a mirror-like soul
to reflect Their radiance,
May the Lords of contract and cosmic law
protect thee,
May ne'er a fruit from Earth's gardens
match the sweetness of the woman that will
love thee,
May all the wise look to thee as their son,
And may thou bring to fruition
the seeds of benevolence
that the Mother and Father of the World
and the All-Embracing,
have set within thee.

Blessing for a Son
By the night that quickens and swells,
shading to purple towards Heaven's Gate
By the comfort, by the heralds of sweet sleep,
May you travel on dreaming wings
to the hinge of the Spirit, deep
Bring out with daybreak,
works woven within
To the eyes of the Sun and a saddened world
Lad, bring forth your dreams.

Visions

The Pattern of the Great Darkness

There the revelation, here as there! Constant and accessible, seated at the base of all sentience. All things are It's appearances, yea, and all imagination is It's breath. The ancients knew It, and within them It shaped It's worldly discourse. Ceaseless has It been, shaping all thought and all religion. Not less true now, not more true then. Incomprehensibly vast and varied, yet the seat taken, all is comprehended. The one Self that plays as all selves, learning to forget, longing to remember, knowing, playing all the while. Truly, this hidden Ultimate is the One Self, as Darkness, invisible, as Mother of the Worlds and as the sentient child at play. Here the revelation, yea, there as here.

The Great Darkness, the Invisible, the Self is one,
and all plurality is It's manifestation.
In truth, the Pattern is mysterious.
It appears to each in accordance with disposition.

Cosmogony in Dialogue

The Seer- I see a grey and lilac expanse of sky. Laced through, it seems, with shimmering points of light. Vast beyond vast. Endless. What is all this?

The Seen- This is the first born. The birthed from the deathless. My Womb. This is the Universe. Not as unmanifest, but at it's primal manifestation. Time is here, but waits. King Saturn is at rest. Invisible here is my Dark Sea. Doubly invisible, the One. Presently, you will witness the birth of my son, fathered by lord Time. Tell me of what you see.

The Seer- I see, rising from the first horizon, a great Sun, effulgent, sublime. A pearl white light, ringed in colours, emanating saffron, pink tinged, carnelian, an opal sphere. All and more.

The Seen - Behold, the birth of the Intellect, the Sun of Creation, my son. Now does the Father stir in my fold. Now does Time commence his dance. Now the Mind begins again it's living. Again, the Cycle has begun it's ascent.

Cosmogony from Silence

Silence
Silence before the Mother,
the Lady of the Lantern
All powerful,
She abides at the base in silence
As silence is at the base of the entire World

Peace
Always, the Ocean of Darkness,
Spiritual, Silent, Eternal, One

Benevolence
Then, rising, the Ball of Light and Sound,
Intelligible, all powerful, the Unity of all

Generosity
Then, the Stars
Creative, intellectual, physical, metaphysical

Compassion
They light up the Great Vault,
all containing, everliving

Peace
Always, the Ocean of Darkness,
Spiritual, Silent, Eternal, One

Oration to the Mother of the Universe

'O Mother of the Universe! O womb that bears and delivers all apparent things! O Maternal Expression of the Holy Absolute! You who are the Substratum of existence, the underlying force that makes manifest the visions of the All-Mind, let our pleas reach even Thee! You are the sentient foundation of All, the fountain of all souls. There, below the whirling landscape of thought wherein the pathways of countless lives lead in wheeling pattern, there You are O Mother, closer in truth than our apparent selves. You are the Creatrix of Being. You are the pinnacle and the depths of the Gods and mortals. It is from You that the phenomenal proceeds. It is within You that the noumenal blooms as all possibility, and it is to the bliss eternal of Your Mind's embrace that every spiral of recurrence finds its paradise and rest.'

O Basileia!

'Pillar of light,
Dawn, Her gown,
Evening, Her mantle
Divinity casting light from Her sea-tower,
All the world, Her reflections, on the still mere of eternity'

The Sacred Night (a vision of the Emanation)

'Always has been the Wakeful Darkness. Self-perceiving, in watchful warmth, is this eternal dark. The Wakeful Darkness is the source of the Mind, and through the transformations of the Mind come the turnings of the universe. Within the Wakeful Darkness appear the Visions, at once perceived and arisen, and these are, through the Creative Intellect of the Mind, translated from out of their dark birthing pool into the myriad forms of the universe. But the turns of the Mind are directed by a flux, the Will, within the Wakeful Darkness. It pulses, now pure, now impure- and thus the character of each cycle gives rise to a universe- now blissful, now painful- in unending wheels of recurrence. When the disturbed phase is ascendant in the Dark, the Mind conceives a painful birth. Herein, the Mind gazes out across the inner abyss of the Dark, and the Will conjures the Mind to fill all inner space with ideation. Thus begins the thoughtful emanation of worlds. The Mind draws Visions from the Dark and casts and establishes them in inner space. Music arises from this great action which causes pain to the Holy Dark which ever loves silence . Thus does tension and unrest arise in the fashioning worlds. Springing in response flows joy and excitement, further distressing the Dark. To restore its peace, from the Dark is thrown up a barrier, and this barrier is Doubt and the Mind braces it.

And so here is a field of restful, comfortable blackness, potent beyond potency, formless, presenting colours and forms. It becomes a vast expanse of darkness, cool and infinitely refreshing. From apparent primordial emptiness, to vast and shadowy space, to the unfolding of the light, energy and mass of the universe and all else, it is a process of disclosure of hidden, or unapparent principle. It is a system of transformation.

The Two Mothers

In the youth of this universe, the Maternal Form, as two visions, passes through Mind. The one is vast in girth, all embracing, and exceedingly great. Her fiery eyes are watchful, Her great arms ever ready to comfort and protect Her mortal young. The other is slender, and shines with a ghostly light- beautiful and utterly chilling- blue baleful eyes searching the stars for a special child with whom to share her elegant misery. And many she finds. Though it often appears to their kin that these ones are blessed and exalted of the universe, in truth their ruinous fate is beyond tears. And while the Great Mother rejoices at the flaming birth of the stars and sets Herself up in cosy observation, the Pale Mother wanders the dark bowels of existence, the dread mountains and haunted plains of the universe, against which gloom her woeful glitter beckons all the stronger.

'hail to the Mother in the hour of pain
All power bestowing
Greater than the Gods
Mistress of all the Worlds'

One Mind, two caves:
one with five gates, the other with six.

Energetic pulses of will, stirring up patterns of regularities from the Deep Mind. That is reproduction.

The Sign of Jupiter Dolichenus (VAUL)

' Four great flowers glow in the night sky - the red and the white, the pink and the purple. Here is glorious VAUL's sign writ large, in this its shape for this painful Cycle of Mind. Lo- the roses glitter in righteous promise for his return beyond the dreadful collapse. In the Hollow of the Dark is the Winged Lord sleeping, among the gods, yea, dreaming in the Deep.

The Turn will come.

We will sleep and awake anew into the Everliving Dream.'

Prayer to the Lady of the Universe

The wind that bears the divine breath, from which all this world proceeds,
flows ever through the caverns of twilight.
Every blessing from the Gods made manifest is this Universe,
From each the forms according to design.
She that is beyond the Gods,
all power from limitless bounty bestowing:
all overflowing from Her through the Gods.
That is all this. How shall we name Her?
She is Hekate , the well of magic,
She is Zeus, the immanent Mind that shapes
She is Apollo , the Lamp behind the Suns
She is Magna Mater, Supreme Mother of the Universe
She is Aion , the keeper of Time
She is Aruru the Dark Womb of the World
She is Athena, the all-pervading Sentience
She is Dolichenus, the power of power,
She is Aphrodite, the love that animates
She is the Realm and the Spirit,
She is the World, the Gods and the mortals,
She is the Living and the Dead,
and That which underlies them both,
She is the Instance and the perpetual.
She is the All in All.
Peace!
She is Indunn, She is Isis
She is Anu, She is Caelestis
She is Urania, She is Rhea
She is Devi, She is Chandika
She is Ninhursag, She is Mammi
She is the Mother of the Gods
She is one with the One

Her Tower
I last saw the Lady of the Tower at the edge of mortal summer.
I saw her lean from a high casement, holding her arms against the warm bricks,
crimson in the final fiery tongues of evening. I left her there, and wandered
through decades half dead, half awake. Soon I will return to her pass again,
retracing my steps, fulfilling the trek of the living vale, aye, in the shadow of her
tower.

The Morrigan says-
Into the Darkness of the Cave of Death, say-
*'Compassion, kindness, gratitude, empathy, love' Say these things and all
names are said. All remembered, nothing forgotten .*

Inis Vohar:

Cole used to run with deer of the forest, spending blissful years, a friend to the
woodland life, a friend to the beasts, a child to the Moon. But the years drew
swiftly past. Cole found he could no longer keep pace with the deer or the fox.
His mind grew weary and his eyes grew dim.

Tired he was of many days mourning friends who had passed before him. Friends
who rose up in happy dawns, shared adventures in the noon times, and faded unto
the dusk. The Moon saw him in greying sadness, the Sun in quiet aching.

Then one evening, a strange wind blew through the boughs, whispering in the
leafy glades, finding Cole at rest. Above the twilight shadows, the early stars
sparked. A voice came to him on that breeze, and it seemed to him a voice of
someone loved, but long forgotten. His old eyes became damp with tears. The
voice spoke –

> *"O, my child, come away with me now!*
> *Silent, have I watched your brief joys*
> *and long hours of sorrow.*
> *All is fulfilled, and nothing ever forgotten.*
> *Know me, for I am thy Mother, and I come to take you home"*

Then Cole felt at last his deepest spirit rising as sleep overtook his old limbs. The
sky seemed to shimmer with twinkling gems of divine colour, and the woods rang
with the sound of crystal bells. On miraculous wings, his spirit took flight into the
bosom of the Night, and passed again into his Mother's embrace, back into the
Eternal Return.

Metirin on the sacrifice (*a vision from ancient Ireland*)

Up among the rocky heights of Mnt Naro is a cave which opens on to the well of Istri. From there flows a stream which joins the great Garun. It is a place monthly sacrifice. Metirin the priest was there one morning with Baru, son of Amgal. Having made a sacrifice to Dian Ceit, the boy questioned Metirin regarding the deity. Metirin spoke thus:

'you see, these Gods and Goddesses are all manifestations of the one we call Dia. They are the forms through which we approach in understanding. Just as one mind extends through countless thoughts, so too does Dia through all of these great ones. Dia is neither male nor female, though we look to embrace it as Mother, for all this that we see is born from Dia, and Dia is as it were, the Womb of the World. As Mother therefore, we have called Dia both Morrigu and Anu: the bearing to life, and the bearing through death. You have heard it said that 'Dargo is all, and Mamlo is Dargo'. Mamlo is the spirit within each of us, in every living thing. In life, all of those individual spirits taken together form the Oenghus, the God of the living. At the death of a living thing, Mamlo regathers all the living-force of that being into himself and assesses the life, waiting to emerge again. Do you see that vapour rising from the sacrifice? That vapour is like the living-force leaving the dead. That living-force is Dargo. It permeates the Universe. An old name for Dia is Dargo! Dia is the person of Dargo. But Mamlo is also Dargo. Therefore, when we sacrifice to Dian Ceit, we are sacrificing to an exalted form of Dia, the one, the formless. Yet Dia is none other than this mysterious living-force that permeates the Universe, the Dargo. And this inner spirit in each of us, Mamlo, is the Dargo. Dia, Mamlo, Dargo. The three are one. That is the great mystery'

The Tuatha De

I saw a lake of bronze water
It was lit by the eternal Sun, which lies as root to the visible.

A company of noble phantoms, garbed in ancient dress, emerged from the sun's rays and marched on feet of mist, whispering across the water. They approached to address me on the shore.

At the forefront was an awesome spectral lord, silver hair swept down like a stream of ice, glorious of countenance, yet harrowed and grave like a hero king of old. Yet kindness was in the flame of his glance. Such unearthly power!

"We greet thee, younger soul. We are the tribe of the god people, the elder children of the Divine Sun, the one Self of all, risen in its own substance, the Womb of Darkness. I am Nuada, and yet you and I are emanations both of that one Self. Look to the Sun, and see our common root made self-visible

Infant of the heavy world, we watch thee, care for thee. Forget us not. Remember our Self and embrace with kindness all the world.
To us you will return. The unity of the Great is beyond earthly unity. It is One beyond number, a unity of which all number is but emanation. Remember us. Remember your Self.

Aon, Ah, Aham, Atman!
Breh, Brigh, Briha, Brahman!"

Then it seemed as if both the sky and the lake sighed, and the mist withdrew with all the kind spirits along with the sky and lake, as if inhaled by the Sun. The Sun then winked shut as an eye falling to sleep, and then indeed there was only the still and sacred Darkness.

The Verses of Comnee
(Spirit of Compassion and succour)
'in gazing at apparent multiplicity
beyond it's window-
The vistas of myriad phenomena
coming and going with the changing light,
So wanders the soul, lost in its own appearances
Placing it's house against a world, and across time
Forgetting that within which is eternally home,
So long does a mortal soul taste sadness
But turning back within,
leaving what vision deems external,
He finds the truth that abides ever in himself
And returns from disparate imaginings,
to that which is ever One'

The Twilight Lesson
"Say along with me, now -
'verily that which is seen, perceived
Verily that which is beyond present sight
In truth what sees and what is seen is One
The Dark is Silence, sentient is the Dark
Filled with the Silent One are all things
All things arise from out the Silent One
The Mindful Dark, the Silent Lights
Myriad, formless and yet only One
To my sister, say I "peace"
To my brother, peace also
From peace come my parents both,
Into the peace shall I return
To the One that is the Night
To the One at Breaking Dawn
The One that is the celestial Gods
That One is also I who call,
Peace , Peace, Peace'

Myth

The Concert of the Great Queen

In the time of dissolution, there is excess and violent division. Not empty is the void for the waves of chaos teem unseen. Then did the Tuatha De struggle against the Fomoiri. Then did the Gods emerge to tie the monstrous ones into order. Vigorous is the battle, Lo-The Dagda sweats. Weary is the striker as he approaches the Great River. -Behold! The Great Queen.

As death hovers above combat, even so, does Morrigu above the war-

Morrigu- join life with death, O Great Father!

By my force comes the victory, even as death is the measure and limit of thy life's abundance. Come, let us unite, and the whirling void will be reordered

The Dagda- Aye! And life's overflowing pulse is the measure and limit of death. Come, we shall reunite.

Etan-From the union of life and death comes the order. Lug is enrobed by the order. Lug becomes the order. Light is the measure of all things.

Morrigu – Aye, but returning into me, even the light.

Eriu speaks-"High as the hills, stronger than the stony mountain on whose side they appeared, I saw the gathering of nineteen lords, and the Great Lady of the Chasm was there behind. These lords, stern some, joyous some (darkly sinister one) were dressed as the ancient greats of Ireland, bearded, armed with silver and gold and in tunics white and yellow. Blue skinned some, and green, two were red and one alone was black. These the nineteen fathers hold the wisdom that is eternal, for through them it flows from the Lady in the Dark. We, the ladies, we will enumerate them. Bres, son of Elatha whom Lug made to proclaim the Law of the Plough, Bres the power of Mighty Brig. Handsome lord, proclaim now, O Bres, some of that wisdom that is eternal"-

Bres speaks- 'the Ocean of Darkness is the Mother, ever present, ever constant. From Her power comes forth this World of multitude, yet it remains ever in Her and of Her- light on the Dark Water, light from the Dark Water.

Brig speaks- 'that light is the Dagda. Just as Bres is the heat of my fire, so is the Dagda the light of the Darkness, and I am the fire of his light.

Boand speaks- 'I am the womb pregnant with that heat. Mananann is my water. Through the light comes forth my son, Oenghus, and Oenghus is life.

Lug speaks- 'I am the friend of Oenghus. I love him and preserve his life. I am the sustaining law.

Morrigu speaks- 'and I am it's fulfilment.

I am the return of all things

Oisin's Gita

A Song for Oisin (of life, death, and return)

1

When it is done
When life in weariness is cast down
She[1] comes on the dark wind and sings
Silent is She, enthroned in Darkness,
showing forth the light of the intelligible stars,
Substratum of the entire Universe,
All-pervading Genetrix
and divine Intellect of the One,

2

Silent, She is, yet speaking-
'Verily, be not dismayed in amazement
that I am both the source of all,
and I am here present, yea, even within thyself.
As the Great Sea of Night shows forth the light of stars,
As the quiet grove at dusk shows forth the evening lamp,
So too is thine own mind in me revealed.
Journey back through the eleven gates,
Journey within to my embrace.'

3

Upon the wings of sleep, I go down,
Into Soul's sky, above the forest of the mind.
In midnight and purple am I wrapped,
To the dell of the first gate, I descend
Behold! In this realm, deception is not easy,
Passions and intentions parade before the view

4

In the daylight of Mind's sun,
The gentle green and radiant realm,
Beneath fragrant growth,
Here the well of the second gate.
Here, it shall be known,
In this place of remembrance,
That here is not You and I,
Though You and I can be seen.

---

[1] The One Consciousness, the Creative Principle, the Mother, the God, the Personified Absolute

6
On the face of Mind's sun
Is the city of the fourth gate
Of ochre and saffron is it's hue,
Here is the realm of the Unity of Powers,
Here is the city of the Creative Gods.

10
Sky of cold rain is the eighth realm
Whose gate is below the red star,
Fly there on the wings of the Lightning Horse,
This realm where Mind's action
Turns to face the Mind.

13
Then, down at the eleventh gate-
Breaking asunder the rocks of Night,
There lifts the veil of time,
Grey is the spray of eternal waters,
The hair of the Woman,
A curtain of flame,
The sound of bells and chimes
And the voice of the Great Sea speaks-

14
(the Goddess)
'Truly, I am all that is,
Of me, you are an infinitesimal part,
Yea, that thou art, but here is a mystery –
An instance of the Self is no less the Self,
I am the Self, and all things are me.
Come now, and we will go back,
Return to the World of Youth,
Back through the Cave of Emergence,
The high house of blue and silver cups
The bowl of the Sun, rose on the waters,
The warm fawn of Elbe,
Come, to turn to re-emerge,
Again and again,
'Till all the hurts of the worlds are healed'

Oracle

Spirit of the Valley and the Pitch Vault of Night

0

0. Beyond the perceptions, the perceiver,
Beyond the perceiver, the intellect,
Beyond the intellect, the lesser self,
Beyond the lesser self, the unmanifest substance,
Enfolding all is the Supreme One.

From the Supreme One, descend the three:
The Force, the Creator, the Sustainer.
These three are the unmanifest substance.
From the unmanifest substance appear
the world, the pattern, and the lesser self,
The pattern, expressed as intelligence,
The world, expressed as perceptions,
The lesser self, expresses as perceiver.
That is this.
One Supreme Spirit.

1

1. The Spirit of the Darkness moves in the valley
It is called both the weaver
and weave of the Worlds
Harmony in dispersal,
filling all the forms,
Heaven's cloth and pattern
endlessly unfurls

2. Through overflowing goodness
the One pulses inward, outward
as this many sided World.
Call the One whatever name seems fitting,
for, through multiplicity, to It all returns
One in all,
All in One.

3. Over the horizon from the primal beyond,
climbs, unwearied, the divine Sun
Radiant Pearl, Creative Sky,
Light of the Self,
fire in the great vault

4. Child, he, of the Great Queen Mother
Fathered by the Silent Tide
Lord of Time, perpetual prince
Saturn the king, in the Mother's fold

5. Blessed this effulgence,
filling vividly the Plain of Power
Land and Loom of the sacred Gods
that the Mother's patterns weave
warp and weft of the waking World,
Aeon's light unfolding,
Rainbow robe adorning
the Hidden, the Invisible,
the One.

6. That which is called being,
is an aspect of non-being,
That which is called non-being,
is an aspect of being.
All exists. Void does not.

7. Void is void, neither a thing nor a nothing.
All exists. Void is not.
In the beginning, there is the Darkness,
and the Darkness is not void.

8. Darkness is not evil :
It is the beginning, the end, the rest, the return.
It is the hidden, the mystery, the nascent realm.
It is the invisible fountain of the visible,
the imperceptible pivot of perceptible change.
In Darkness there is faith, peace, and promise

9. Darkness inheres in light,
unconsciousness in the conscious.
Light and consciousness expressions both
of the Great Unexpressed.
To that they return.
From that they arise anew.
That is the Way.
If there is another, then that too is the Way.
Outside of the Way, there is not.
From Darkness to light,
from unconsciousness to consciousness,
from death to immortality.
That is the Way of the realization of the Self.

1. One source and all containing!
Axle, Pivot, and Culmen of creation.
Invisible, Darkness,
yet also Primal Light and Person.
One, and Polarity too!
Yet, only One.

2. A Unity beyond number,
but all things are Their manifestations.
All worlds are Their form,
yet are They formless.
All minds are Their Mind,
and yet are They ruler.
All lives are Their life,
and yet are They deathless.
Time is Their action, Divine is Their nature.
Their's is the Ultimate Substance.

3. From One does the all come forth,
Into One does the all return.
I am nothing but what I am in Them.

4. Know the Supreme Invisible,
the Great Ultimate,
the Wakeful Darkness,
the Self upon which
all the patterns of the Universe
are given forth, woven,
the Hidden Pivot of all perceptible change.
Ultimate, yes, and fully present
in each and every instance, individual.
This All is in each, as each is in the All.

1. The cause is in the effect,
is the effect not also within the cause?
The One is oneness, all that is is one.
All things are all things
and all things are one.
Between the oneness of the One,
And the oneness of all things,
there you will find the hinge of the Spirit

2. As the Spirit, you will see without effort,
and let the worlds rise and fall,
like foam and bubbles,
rising from the night sea.

1. Distilled from the infinite is the finite
Distilled from the perpetual is the temporal
From what is distilled the infinite, the perpetual?
Verily, from the Eternal, verily from the One

2. Born from death is life,
Born from beginning is the end
Born from what, is death, the beginning?
Verily from the imperishable,
verily from the Real
Born from earth is the air,
Born from fire is the earth,
Born from water is the great fire
And divine is the breath of the Darkness,
Yea, and Spirit is It's consciousness.

3. Heaven and Earth are parents to the myriad
All are enfolded by Heaven and Earth
All beings, one family with Heaven and Earth
all of one substance, forming one body.

4.Truly, all this is the Beautiful, the Highest!
Heaven, Earth, and the myriad form three,
yet all are the Beautiful,
and the Highest Beauty is One.

1. Exist on the horizon from which
the million millions arise.
Gaze outward and inward onto infinite space.
Rest in the still mere from out which pours
the cycles of Time's stream.
Embrace in love the self in all beings,
all beings in the Self.

2.Established in darkness is the light,
Cast forth from heat is the cold
On what support, the darkness, the heat?
Verily, the invisible, verily the Self.

3. Formless, yes, all forms in potentiality.
Eternal, yes, time held in hidden coils-
designs, pathways, epics, victories,
all elements to unfold,
or to remain hidden
One, yes, all numbers residing,
uncounted, unuttered.
Alone, yes, alone, Self-sufficient, Real.
Absolute, yes, manifesting
as subject and objects.
This is That.
From, on, in That- darkness, light, colours.
From, on, in That- life, death, immortality
From, on, in That- mind, matter, motion.
Person, aye! Person, Principle, both, neither, All.

1. Seeming cold, empty, vast,-
unlovely, the frontier, forth from which,
the lamps of living bring light, growing heavy
Pitch deepened, the ravine
erupting the swell

2. Silent, enthroned in Darkness,
Showing forth the lights of the intelligible stars
Substratum, Creatrix of the whole World
Divine Intellect and Power from the One
Mightiest, She
The Mother of the Universe.

3. From Her the Universe rises,
Into Her, the Universe dissolves
She is called the Mother of the worlds,
Verily, the Self as Mother of all things.
There is no Universe besides the Self,
The One is all,
and the Self is One.

4. Silent, Dark, is She,
keener than the Father's flame,
enduring beyond the Hero's deed,
closer than the dreamer's dream,
the stillness of ground, supporting the Way,
the Night presenting stars,
the Mother of life, of worlds,
of space.

1. From the first-lit Horizon of Dream come all,
Dreaming the World,
flower blooms from the Dark stream
In Whose Mind, all this: the play of aeon's light?
Verily, the Mother,
fertile Channel of the Deep Might

2. Invisible in Dream,
Invisible in waking life,
Intuition views the margin
From which all things arise

3. Strong, unfolding all as Light,
Universal hinge
Casting forth all temporal things
The Hidden Ultimate
Source and pattern of the worlds

4. Where do I meet Her?
All the within, all the without.
Fully present is Her pattern,
Moon before Moonrise

5. From It, Time is suspended,
In Time, all things arise and dissolve,
Time, and light, and million millions,
Into Itself, the Dark Womb withdraws.

8

1. The Substratum dreamed a world,
The world dreamed life,
Life dreamed a body,
The body dreamed a person,
The person dreamed and died,
The dream, then, returned
to the Substratum, as a memory,
To be brought to mind again
Rising, and falling anew

2. Truly, the mind of Heaven
is the storehouse of mysterious idea.
Whatever exists is not truly contingent

3. Not all the wealth and power
of the human world
can manifest a single natural life
Not all of that wealth and power
can atone for it's wanton destruction
Be mindful,
for verily, is Heaven mindful

4. Be mindful not to threaten,
Let threatening depart from all our minds,
That is a good step towards the great clearness,
That is the Way of humanity
Refined to the Heavenly Way.

1. Ah!
I see, star-lit, in Heaven's chambers high,
Jupiter the King, and all the blessed Gods,
Exalted they, forms of the One,
the True, the Self,
Children of the Mother,
base and Womb of the World

2. Ah!
The Great Sun of Creation
Rises again over the Hill of Elbe
Radiant tide, light flooding
the plain of the Gods, eternal
All filling this brief self of becoming
Splendid, mighty,
kind are they

3. From the sunlit place,
this mortal has gone forth
May he have served them
May he have remembered them
May he see them again,
on his return.

4. Marvellous is all this, the Universe,
manifest of the mind of the Great Mother,
Dreamer of the everliving dream
on the silent waves of eternal Night

5. Towers of vision rise up,
of obsidian waters composed,
Repeating, repeating,
perpetual thrusts
So bloom the worlds,
So they wilt,
and return

6. All nature here is enfolded
Yea, the seeming unnatural too
For the Womb of Mind outward pulses
and in all directions withdraws

1. She sees in apparition,
the pink-rosed Fountain
of Universal Springs
Ceaseless it plunges and strikes up again,
The Waters of Worlds' Births
deathlessly renewed

2. She sees, pulsing in the Dark
the universe again, ever refreshed
Hills and houses rising against Dawn's sky,
In the plains and fields, beasts on the hoof,
Turquoise bunting, fluttering in the breeze,
in a return'ed realm beneath the sun.

3. He sees laid out anew the plains of summer,
the holy crescent and the homes,
a light in the hall
when the night sails high
In the sacrosanct sky-
the horns, the lamp
and all of the stars

4. I see, swelling up again, the old world,
- warm as the womb
A green-leafed languor
of a bright late spring,
at eventide the promise of summer's approach
The adorable mantle of the Eternal Being-
The world as it was
and will be again

5. On wings, and I see an island warm,
a bird, yellow plumed
and a white town
By a mountain great I see
myself and all other selves around
I see an end to fear,
I see a home of hope

6. I see a nighted world,
rising, most familiar
The shapes of dear things,
from the shadows ascending
I see a jewel of Puce in the sky
and I hear a voice
that I have always known

7. I see a garden,
damp and overgrown,
the heavy scent of generation around
I sense a pulse everliving within
I see a glass and in reflection,
See I

8. I see that other world
under Time's Eye, far and near,
City dark, the granite and ground
from Mind's triple casement appear

9. I see the dome of sparkling stars,
life's true water, incomparably blue,
I sense the violet cloud arise,
the endless story,
old and new.

10. Here I see, an ocean of life,
rising forever, from out the Dark Sea.
In cycles unending, breathing men and beasts,
as a pillar of wind on the morning air

11. Here, I see a black watered pool
with a fire at its centre, blazing without fuel
Up in a whirling tower, worlds rise and fall,
as sparks against the pitch vault of night

'I am all that is, that was, that will be again
Yea, though the mortal mind
Pierces not my shadow'

'I am the content and the vessel,
I am the turns of space and the stars,
I am the Dawn and the Dusk,
Mother of the Sun,
We are the Dark beneath Daylight'

1. I saw, through the door of dream,
a world gone still and quiet
Soft sighs of crumbling bones
Far off whispers of falling dust
Little stirs, achingly remote
One star at nightfall
but no living eye to see
Silence for a long age.
The Spirit turns in the Dark of Space

2. I saw in dream, an eclipse –
a Sun emerging greater,
A storm's black pall come menacing,
Yet, swiftly vanishing away

Some prophets thrill seeing doom,
- not so this seer of worlds
A morn of mist and midday may,
But night wells whispers of new shoots

I see, risen up again –
The towers of smiling women and men,
Garlands of song, from roof to roof
Bells of crystal,
Dawn in Tara, green.

Oracle of One Mind

In the darkness beneath thought
Creativity and will are one
The nature of self-and-world is one
Extending creatively
from the darkness beneath thought

In the lofty heights of Cosmic Consciousness
As sentient lights, all things are gathered,
Each resting on the three aspects
Watchers are they of the Supreme Axle's production
As worlds within One Mind only

All minds are bound to the One Mind,
for consciousness contains the substance of creation
and creation exists not apart from consciousness
For consciousness and creation are mutually interpenetrated
With consciousness is creation bound,
animating the world with soul
With consciousness is creation bound,
the seer and seen as one, as the World

This pattern is the root of discrimination
Creation is the process of discrimination
Creation is sustenance for the discursive intellect
Utterances concerning the pattern
Describe it as ineffable before Heaven arises
Ineffable, yea, and silent

Blessed is life, flowing forth
from Heaven to Earth
Felicitous, constant is the principle of life
Proceeding from the culmen of One Mind
Divine creativity and pattern

The One Mind with indescribable sound,
with total understanding all multifaceted ideas,
outward flowing as a heavenly fountain
For from One Mind is willing and fulfilling
Divided according to pattern
By noetic fire established
By the pattern of One Mind proceeds the World

As a river of heavenly creation,
the Mother resides as generative fire
For the primordial remains totally pure
And as concrete existence by consciousness proceeds
For the primordial is One Mind as Mind
Weaving creative fire with fire
While preserving the finest fire as Mind

Thence a whirling tower of flame,
drawing down from the finest fire
Sparkling as all the phenomena of the worlds
Downwards extending as radiance sublime

As a heavenly fountain, the Principle whirls
Ceaseless motion as effortless rest
The Principle bound close to One Mind
Manifesting as concrete forms and transformations,
Being the processional Way
between One Mind and Nature
Shaping as concrete images the thoughts
As the World those thoughts become

All minds are bound to the One Mind,
for consciousness contains
the substance of creation
And creation does not
exist apart from consciousness
For consciousness and creation
are mutually interpenetrated
With consciousness is creation contained,
animating the world with soul
With consciousness is creation contained,
the seer and seen as one, as the World

Allegory

The Desolation

In the northern darkness on a desolate shore, a dying old man slipped into dream.
The spirit of the sea rose and in whispers questioned him-
"Why are you left here alone to die on these despairing sands? where are your
children, your women and kinsfolk gone"
in dream, he answered-
"the rocks came alive and devoured the women, the pirates from the south stole
the children away, the men slew each other in grief. That is all"
The sea replied -"nothing wholly false, nothing wholly true-
Long have I watched and know well the truth of your people's dearth. Your fields
were exhausted- rocks, alone remaining: and so your women were suffered to die.
Your children were taken indeed: but in truth, it was you that sold them. Your
kinsmen hacked each other down: but in the rage of unsatisfied greed, not grief.
Greed was the vice that turned your fields to stone, greed sold your children, greed
slew your kin. Greed had your devotion. Grief is your reward. I will bear your
fateful tale in my waters to centuries hence. Sleep now, for verily is Death greedier
than thee"

From the Corpse of the Great Snake

'I see:
having grown in gut of the Great World-Snake
Little lords of greed,
They spring now from her side.
Rebellion in the air, maybe,
but watch for those with wealth increase:
-Loud in their support, long have they prepared!-
Leading with plans laid-
let theirs be first blood drawn!
Aye, the great snake lies now:
self-slain dead
Let these new-sprung lords of greed
to downfall's doom
follow first'

The Kracken

'Behold! Mighty Leviathan, Kracken the Great!
risen in a jet of filthy cloud!
Tentacles clutching the ship of human progress,
its triple-beak slavering in the gore of its feast.
On deck, the people turn in the madness of fear to rage,
hating, blaming, trampling the other,
running to life-boats, flying each a different flag,
Hasty in hope of flight to home-shores
Poor souls: upon the world ocean, yet will they be bound-
alone, will each be devoured in turn
Now in inky effluent
the beast drags the great craft into the boiling swell.
Disunity, aye-
dismembered by passion, fear, by false design
So sinks the ship of human progress
Yet, verily now
will all be devoured
alone'

The Serpent

I followed the gleam of a pale moon to a cemetery. At it's centre appeared to rise a
great pillar, a shadow against the green lunar light. I approached, and saw that it
was not a pillar, but an immense serpent, hideous, with eyes of jet,
it's lolling tongue blue, dripping venom.
Forking to point east and west.

A low moaning echoed from the rotten soil, for the dead were not at rest. Poor
souls!-they were troubled still by the stinking poison which lay gathering in pools,
soaking through the grim earth beneath the monstrous viper. Unseeing though the
eyes of the beast were, nonetheless, I knew it was ware of me.
The surface of the right eye shimmered in an insane light-
unwholesome, hateful.
That of the left reflected dully the disc of the moon as a hollow phantom-
lifeless, empty.

I knew then that all those now lying dead had been drawn from either side,
towards an eye,
there to drink deadly deceit from the tongue.
No other choice had been presented them.

The grinning countenance of the abomination spelled out in my thought
"Here be truth"

The dead groaned beneath my feet
" heed it not. It lied".

The Angler-fish

'then I saw in my dream, a demon angler-fish of terrifying girth
It approached the Earth, gaping wide with globe-swallowing maw
It shimmered in luster of silver, gold, and black
Blind were it's deathly eyes of pearl, scorching the air venting from its gills
The people of the Earth stood armed to resist it – but lo
Upon it's blood-curdling head, a lure to divide it's foe!
Capitalism this monsters true name, yea
Though "globalisim" spelled it's deceitful lure
One monstrosity, two faces, true and false,
No heart
One deadly mouth'

The Shark

I saw in my dream, the ocean boil in bloody froth
Raising it's head, a monstrous fish, gore stained
A mouth with three rows of daggers white.

The first and outer set: broken and worn from it's kills,
the name of 'Christ' scrawled across them.

More in tact, the second, less blunted they were:
upon these was carven 'Woke'.

The third, pristine and waiting-
deadly sharp!-they gleamed out letters spelling 'Nation'.

Ever hungry, insatiable for the flesh of man.
The beast plunged again and hurried towards the shoreline
where played the children of the world,
heedlessly in the surf

Elbe

THE SEERESS OF ELBE

(*this is an imagined dialogue between the mortal self and the principle of wisdom innate within the mortal consciousness, personified as the "Seeress"*)

This I remember- that flying in dream my mortal-self drifted along low sea-walls by a salt marsh at dusk. To the right, the sea, to the left, the dour expanses of the marsh. At a certain distance, a troubling whirlwind loomed. Then a sacred guide appeared as a phantom woman, and led me to a great portal, shimmering like wheel of sapphire light. Through this was revealed the way of heaven, a hill-road towards a darkened sky. This is how it was unfolded.

'At last, ascending the high hill of heaven, I found the grotto and green bower, in which her lantern was lighted, blessed lady wisdom, internal ground of groundless consciousness, mother-gate to and from the Supreme. Listen!

It was asked[2]- "*What is the nature of the Divine?*"

The seeress replied- "*what answer would satisfy you? All of these names and forms – Brahman, God, Buddha, Heaven, Sakti, Christ, Zeus, Isis. All of these, and more than all yet formed, by mouth, in mind. What of them? On the northern slope of that hill yonder, there appears a faint shadow at midday. If I told you that that shadow is the Mother and Father of the Worlds[3], would you believe it? And yet, were it possible for you to investigate it to the utmost, you would find it to be so, and exhaust your person in the doing . Better to just believe, for believing is a kind of knowing. The root of believing and knowing is not non-existent. Call it what you wish, but whenever you say "I", you glance at its presence. That is all. For further expressions of this truth, consider these passages :*

PRINCIPLE OF DARKNESS - *A great darkness encompasses all that is, even as It generates it, preserves it, reclaims it- a fathomless sentience, of which the mortal consciousness is but a focusing instance. A dynamic in unity, a Principle of principles, Self and Self-emptying in inexhaustible abundance. Self-emptying to experience Themselves as phenomenal selves. Some see in It the face of God, yet, verily, unfathomable is this groundless ground on which appears God, the Soul, and the World: One, Absolute, and Formless Sentience. Generosity, love, Unity. Often painful, yet always good. That is this*

---

[2] By the mortal self, the objectified 'I'
[3] The Absolute being present at the root of all things, even a vague a fleeting shadow

The Self -*Witness how all the worlds rise from me, have me as their base, and know that into me, shall they all melt away- indeed! Thou know'est, thou perceive'th not the dynamics of thine own body, from out which thy vision opens. How much less dost thou see as the foundation, though it resides within as thine own self.*

Consider- *Mystery is the weave of the cloth of Heaven, Doubt is it's dye, and Beauty is it's purpose. There is nothing more in this for reason to address*

For, *Heaven and earth bring forth the multitude of things according to principles, some of which are mysterious. All that appears is so by the actions of Heaven and earth. All is natural, even though unnatural seeming. The one, over-arching principle, of which all that appears is the manifestation, the Principle of principles, is also within all it's appearances. Though it can be experienced, apprehended, yet it is beyond description in words.*

Say-**"Heaven and Earth are parents to all the multitudes, including this tiny, brief form I have found myself in. All are enfolded by Heaven and Earth. Therefore, all beings are one family with Heaven and Earth, and all are of one substance, one great body. Truly, all this is Brahman, and this self within is Brahman. Heaven, Earth and the million millions are three, yet all are Brahman, and Brahman is One."**

The Dynamism-*There are three great exhalations of the divine breath. One producing all phenomena. One harmonising all phenomena. One sets the self-animation of the self-animated. All from the divine breath, which is the divine sound, and that sound is identical to the divine Self. A World once arisen is a world that will return. Unending are the wheels of recurrence.*

The Spirit -*There are strata to the world, yet all exist within the One Spirit. That Spirit exists within, as the foundation of all. I rested on the heavenly hill, the high point in the world of spirits. What did I perceive? A great and invigorating wind forever washes through that misty world. There, innumerable spirits stand watching: sharp, alive, yet peaceful. In the sky above, the winds resolve and are breathed out again by a pale Sun, the image of the divine in that world. That is the culmen of the spirit world. There the spirits choose when and where they will descend into physical life again.*

The Mind -*The mind pervades all things, is the one consciousness which hears, sees, cognises through myriad forms, and the self is the ruler of the mind. The world is as inseparable from the mind as is the heat from the fire. Seek thou to know the ruler of the mind.*

Seek to realize the one Self.
The idea of the Great Self can be likened to the sea,
though nothing can be likened to the Great Self.
The physical is the surface- the waves of this sea of consciousness.
The Spirit is the substance, the water.
The Deity is the currents.
The world-dynamic is the tide.
The Great Self is the absolute
Spirit is It's substance.
The World is It's function.

Nature-*A human life can be considered a gift.*
A human body can be considered an attainment.
The gift is the providence of Heaven,
The attainment is of the Ruling Principle of nature,
Neither are the remit of the individual person.
Therefore, one should thank Heaven for life, should honour the attainment with respect and
grateful heart, should engage them both by becoming truly human. That is the remit of the
individual person. By becoming truly human, one realizes the Unity of Heaven, Nature, and all
the individual things. That is Divine Unity.
It was asked- *"what then is evil?"*

The seeress replied-*"see here, rising from the void on a heavy cloud,*
a monstrous head with two faces-
one of ice, one of fire,
The one of ice answers to the name of 'Apathy'
The one of fire, 'Cruelty'
This is the one spirit of evil that haunts the human world-
one spirit, two faces.
There grows no evil apart from this canker.
Worship it not. Shelter it not."

It was asked-*"and what of the great cloud on which it rises?"*

The seeress answered-*"that cloud is called 'ignorance'*

The Other -*The Other is the Self's reflection, it is the polarity within One. There is no need to*
transcendentalise the Soteron

It was asked of the Seeress- how should one self-identify in a world obsessed with identity?

The Seeress replied -
At the beginning of an aeon a great black dog, immeasurably vast, though invisible, feels the bite of a flea behind it's ear, and motions itself to scratch. From first reaction to the rending of the itch, and the flinging off of the flea, a hundred thousand billion eras pass. Meanwhile, on the back of that flea, a world forms, and brings forth life. People are born and fill their lives with conflict and cruelty, believing their engagements to be of foremost moment. They toil and bind onto themselves a bric-a-brac of cobbled identities. They fight, and swing from day to day in painful clamour. How unhappy. How unnecessary.

Verily, all is Spirit. Know thyself as but an instance of such.
Seek this perspective, for as the Spirit,
you will see without effort,
and let the worlds rise and fall, like foam and bubbles,
rising and dispersing from the night sea.

How to conceive of the Spirit's work?
'From the Northern Cloud of Oblivion to the Southern Lake of Darkness, a bolt of brilliant lightning flashes forth every hundred thousand billion aeons of perpetual time. In that flash, is all that is, has been and will be of this world's life. From darkness to heavenly darkness. What then the need for such strife?'

If I say " I am Great Emperor Darkness" and you say the same, then we are near to memory. Then we are near to truth. O mortal! Find a time of silence and seek out a secluded place. Intending to memory, think upon this : the Universe is one, and myriad are it's manifestations. The Absolute is one, and all abides within.

It was asked of the Seeress- "What is this existence?"

She answered –
It is One. One beyond number,
One encompassing all.

"Truly, all this is the Beautiful, the Highest! Heaven, Earth, and the myriad form three, yet all are the Beautiful, and the Highest Beauty is One.

Look to the northern sky at night, the culmen of the starry vault. It is the book of the field of Heaven. It's patterns are coloured by that which reads them.

The Great Celestial Presence is the awesome, the encountered in original perception. It may be the beginning of inspiration, it's first stimulant, but it leads to the inner encounter. The inner encounter is the fundamental. It is an uncovering. It leads to a recognition of the Supreme Unity

From the Beginningless arises the beginning. Time stirs with presentation, and presentation arises in the Mind. Which is first? Time, Presentation and the Mind: these three are profoundly intimate. Though dialogically distinct, they are a unity. The three are mutually implicated. This is the Primal Constitution.

Together with the Beginningless, this Primal Constitution is called Spirit. Spirit, invisible, is both immanent and transcendent. The Mind of Spirit is immanent as the Great Pattern, and the Universe is it's manifestation.

All apparent causes are relations within being. The set of all causes, the centre of the web of interrelations is the Supreme Immanent, the Great Pattern- being itself. The transcendent aspect of the Mind of Spirit looks both at the Universe, and back into the Beginningless.

The Great Pattern of being includes the pattern of the human mind. Thus, the human mind is an instance of the Supreme Immanent.

Therefore, in it's transcendental aspect, the human mind is a door to the other world. That door is represented by the Great Celestial Presence. All within the Supreme Unity.

Know this: that which is manifest here, has passed through all forms, and will pass through them again and again, in the overflowing bounty of time Yea, perpetual time.

'When it is the dynamic of the Universe,
it is called Nature.

When it is inherent self-consciousness in the dynamic,
it is called Soul.

When it transcends the particulars of time and extension,
it is called God.

These three names refer to the same,
which is called Spirit'

THE CLOUD AND THE ABYSS (the Seeress of Elbe part 2)

I asked in dream, the unseen ground,
as to the nature of all that is.
By ways, it was answered :
"A violet cloud appears in the abyss. Each vaporous particle reflected in each, so that there is only one essence, One presented as myriad. It transforms according to it's own principles. It rests in darkness, though in constant motion. Without this cloud, there is no abyss. Without the abyss, there is no cloud. The abyss, the cloud, and the myriad transformations : they are distinct, yet they are One."

Then the Seeress appeared,
from the star-flecked ground of the holy abyss,
cyan and mauve,
on midnight blue, her woven shawl,
ascending her throne of augury.
She speaks –

THE ABYSS
Behold, be embraced by the dawning abyss!
the Great Darkness,
overflowing yet inexhaustible
Empty of all relative things, disclosing them all,
To this they return, never having left
Full and Absolute,
One
and
Eternal

PRINCIPLE OF LIGHT
One is the Supreme Light of heaven and earth!
A glittering star, a lamp on the universal tree,
without fire, it glows
from the blessed effulgence of the oil itself
Light of the light is the One
Wisdom of all things, shining
Of whom light and darkness are as twin gates
From out which floweth the world as a forked river
One Mind through two doors
That is all this

PRINCIPLE OF THE SUPREME CONSCIOUSNESS
The Supreme Consciousness, which focuses Itself in myriad instances as mortal consciousness to experience It's inherent creativity as and in the world It generates from Itself, contains, envelops, supports the world – all worlds. It therefore is both self-limited and Supreme.

The Seeress of Elbe pt 3

The Seeress then led me through my minds abyss,
to a vast expanse, shrouded in night.

The ground was soaked underfoot, a quagmire black, heaving beneath
impenetrable shadow.

Behold! in the distance, a flicker of blue fire, risen, vanishing like a ghost of a
dream near waking.

'that fire you see' **she said**
'in that gout of flame, a hundred billion cycles of the your Universe. In a hundred
billion years of our time here, will it blaze forth again, and so on and on. All that
you have known: recurring billions in just one flash, billions of flashes on this dark
and eternal bog.
As it is said :

'Here I see, a black watered pool,
With a fire at its centre, blazing without fuel
Up in a whirling tower, worlds rise and fall,
As sparks against the pitch vault of night'

The Seeress of Elbe pt 4

'The Seeress led me then from the gate of night to a fragrant bower. She pointed, and I saw a fallen folly: the Temple of the Sun. The violet beds and scented herbs were strewn with its rubble.

She spoke-
"see here a doomed project:
a vain man laid the foundation,
deceitful men and women raised it's lower tier,
gullible the many that thought to build it up"

"I and many others tried to warn them" **I said**

Spake she - "Aye many, and you failed. You could not gauge the depth of their suffering, those born after you. They craved adopted phantoms. The world demanded of them identity. The world would not accept what the same world had raised in them. To sell their selves, to buy acceptance, they stitched upon themselves the empty ghosts of words and idols and called it tradition. A painful fashion, born of pain, by pain sustained, through pain expanded. They heaped the pain of their unease, one onto the other as cults in all but name. Poor souls. But peace to them now. They will rest and renew.

Explanation
The weaving of new mythologies, the fashioning or refreshing of ideologies is a creative tool for humanity in facing crises.

While the natural substratum of humanity's existence has been relatively stable, the complexity of such abstractions has been able to grow to the extent where near transcendence of the environment has been reached: near, but in not being reached, it is bound to be drawn back to realization of the immanence of the Earth in mortal life. An incomplete transcendence is a phantom, and a dangerous mirage.

And the substratum is no longer stable. That presages either a return and revitalisation of the philosophy of immanence, oriented towards holism, or the last battle of phantom armies with real weapons shedding living blood on a parched or flooded landscape where new species of disease and parasites will constitute the only locus of thriving growth. Hunger and hordes of winter vermin before a swift decline through war and calamity.

Chase phantoms- then blood, fire and pestilence.
No new myths need be woven to reveal that as true.

Hymn

Hymn to Isis

One is the Divine Mother,
Whose Being shows forth as million millions,
One is She Whose Sentient Womb swells the Universe,
Dark Waters, Light bearing- Mother of Time, Father of Life
Tree, Whose precious flowers
Enshrine the faces of all the Gods,
Pattern and weaver of the Worlds,
Maternal Substratum of existence,
Isis, Queen of Heaven and Earth

'Silent, enthroned in Darkness,
Showing forth the lights of the intelligible stars
Substratum, Creatrix of the whole World
Divine Intellect and Power from the One
Mightiest! She
The Mother of the Universe.
To Her, Say- "Thou art all that I am, Yea! And more.
I am nothing but what I am in You"'

One is the Real, the Absolute
One alone, appearing as million millions
Omnipotent, One alone
One Spirit, many faces

Ninhursag

Meditate ye on That one fountain,
Sublime, self-luminous, foundation of the World,
Which rises from the Dark Deep of the Star Mother,
Lady of the Cycles,
She Whom is the Soul of the Universe,
She That gazes upon Herself,
whenever a being opens their eyes,
All encompassing Matrix
from Which, water, fire, and earth appear,
Lady Tower of the wind,
Mother, Daughter,
and Mind of the
Sentient Night

Ninhursag

Here beneath all, rise the Pillars of the World
Opal posts, high tower peaks, unshakable support
Restful abode of cool breezes
Castle of Aether, Timeless City,
Precious, it's ceilings, imperishable vault,
Jasper, yea, and amethyst,
Turquoise, mauve, carnelian,
Musk scented is the shrine,
Domed by the Eye of Time,
Hall porch of the shining one,
Mother and Queen and Cosmos,
Watcher of Her Worlds
Light ripples, Her raiment
Tremors from unbounded silence
Yet, ever still are Her depths,
Her flood, the swelling universe
As tides of light flow, wavering
She wears the Crown of Powers
The governorships of all the Gods
Gathering, dispensing, motionless,
Heart of Bliss, is She
Sublime Cavern,
Birthway of the Sun

Daughter of the Dawn

O, Sun and air, chamber of rose,
Winding path of the Lady of the Turn
Glad is the high breeze
Sweet as crystal dew
that murmurs through,
the sky lane of her descent
Gently whispering,
Beloved of Day and Night,
Who brings sleep and reawakening,
on each blessing palm

Hymn to the Eye of Mercy
(Horus)

'I see a tear like a star in the Dark,
The Eye of Mercy, eternally bright
I see a hammer of crystal in Dream
The Divine Family Of infinite Care.
Spirit of the Stars
Spirit of the waters
Spirit behind the Aions
Spirit of my soul

Grianu

Oh, beautiful divine Sun,
Son of the life-giver, born of the Dark
Immortal among the mortals,
Friend of friends on Earth
Beautiful one, thee I love
Stir in our souls,
as rays of thy light,
to turn in benevolent affection towards each,
For the enlivening of earth's pulse,
yea- the quickening of Heaven's stream.

Hymn to Sarapis

As the raiment of the Darkness,
You are Dawn,
Sarapis is Your son,
His moisture is abundance
in sleep, go to His holy place
On the wings of dream
to His house in the earth
Joyous is His house
and He fills the earth with joy
He, whom three sisters raised
He, the eternal Child,
He resides as perfection
He is abundant in life and death
His fire brings completion
His heat brings reawakening

Hymn to Epona

Higher rises the mare
Upon the shoulders of the Twins
stalking the courses of the sky
High over the plains of night,
hear Her battle cry
Troubles of the weary lives
She casts beneath Her wheel
Before a red morn, pray to Epona

Hymn to Saturn

'Lord of the Silence,
all things dissolved in Thee
Father of the Gods is Your Son,
The Mind before reason's toil art Thou,
Horned King, observer of the silence,
Essence before motion art Thou ,
Through You, does the all return,
Silent King of the Great Sea.

Verse to Silvans

'and he raises his forehead,
Old King Pinewood in the North sky,
A Blue Boy climbing the hill road of Heaven
A tremor of Dawn,
And the Puce Globe approaching '

Miscellaneous

Such as is
Mind as mirrored water
with freshened heart as snow
See, flickering in the matchless fire:
depthless dark and infinite light
a formless union-
One, Supreme, and Real

Hidden is the storehouse-
seeds of light and dark, shining
Sublime, all-embracing,
Foundation in eternity.

The Supreme Mystery : one unchanging Reality, flickering as phenomenal change.

Waiting
'Life has flown past me, -away
as a dream between darkness and memory
Thoughts as the glittering of evening dew
Heaven reflecting
Mind before the Moon'

One Great Family

(a meditation)

When I was younger, in childishness,
I wanted a son and daughter

Now, without children of my mortal self's own
I must regard all sons as my son, all daughters my daughter
All fathers, my father, mothers my mother, brothers, sisters all

This brief self of becoming
which I call my own
is but a phantom of light and shadow,
a whisper, a shimmer, a surface tremor
of a great and wide,
A world-bearing water.

For there is only one true Self
One, and One only
Of One, we are all,
but murmurs, shadows
tremors in water and light

The Bright Death Comes
'Rising on the horns of a new moon, I see
A bright death riding, a dawn before dawn
In the east, a deadly sun
burnt offerings on the western plinth
A bright death, under evening
darkly creeping, dead by night'

Sough
'I see a world of snow and ash,
white wings in the star-vault,
cold air, gone still,
I hear-
Creation's new soughing,
a hum from the fathomless
I know now the cycle's turn is near'

Valley
'I see, in violet blooms again-
the midday vale, in God and space,
Mother, father,
brotherhood and love,
Beyond the death
and night's embrace'

The Siren in the Dark
Behind the phenomena-
the Field of Darkness
Behind that Darkness-
the Other World
From Sentient Darkness
and the Eternal Sound
Arise the worlds
In the Pattern round

Diagram of the Great Darkness
To the North, the Door of Heaven
To the South, the Door of the Living
To the East, the Door of Night,
To the West, the Door of Day
The fifth, all-embracing!
The Supreme Axle of Heaven and earth
Culmen and the base,
The Great Spirit, the individual spirit.
All within the Great Darkness.

The Body of the Universe,
the Mind of the Universe,
the Self of the Universe.
The Manifestation,
the Pattern-Principle,
the Way.
Six aspects, two faces.
One and Absolute.

The Supreme Culmen

At the Culmen supreme, I know
there is the root of Heaven and Earth
In celestial haze, under eyes- black and starlit
Beyond which, nothing-
but eternal within

as it is said -
"The jeweler looks on his shadow
Blue warm the moon, over the tunnel it dips
Peace in the hearths and the homelands
Rafters arise over Elbe"

Supreme Culmen, visible, invisible
Darkness before days and nights
All potent sentience before reason's toil
Vault, apex, middle sea,
and substratum of all worlds

Change

1

UNDIFFERENTIATED

'The phenomenal is (by the mind), the differentiated and dispersed.
The noumenal is the undifferentiated, whole.
Being undifferentiated, it is pure.
Being pure, it is unlimited, powerful.
Being unlimited, powerful,
it is at the source of change, motion.
Being at the source of change, motion,
it can be the sanctuary of rest.
Being the sanctuary of rest,
it can be the well of re-energising, refreshment.

**Before the seer, the seeing, and the seen-
before the three nodes of waking experience
is the undifferentiated.
In being undifferentiated, it is ineffable.
In being ineffable, it is outside of time and spatial
limitation.
And yet it is omnipresent,
immanent at the base of mortal mind.
Draw your awareness there.
It is a fount of potency and security.**

2

PATTERN

The Great Darkness, the Invisible, the Self is one,
and all plurality is It's manifestation.
In truth, the Pattern is mysterious.
It appears to each in accordance with disposition.
The structure, in experience of day and night.

The authentic attainment of a human is to embody
humanity/humaneness
Nature has enfolded this,
and the human mind can unfold as this.
The Universe embodies the Principle of nature in its
majesty, vastness, and generation of life.
The human embodies the Principle of nature
in becoming humane.
The Universe makes present.
The human makes ascent,
in the ways particular to the person.

3

<u>PARENT</u>

Upon the flow of life's true water are bound the stories of the World. Streaming from the Great Queen, enthroned in the Halls of Night. She is the Sun of Water, She is the Ocean of Light. Silent and loving, She: Mother, Queen and Cosmos.

The love of parents buoys up life. The love of parents, so strong! think then on the love of the Mother of the Universe! Believe it, for even if thou believe it not, yet is it true. Let love be a sign for you, the weave of Her gown, the current of the Heavenly River, the Tide of the All Encompassing Sea.

Personality is also founded on principle: the manifesting of elements, the gathering together of elements, to form personality is also there, co-extensive with the personality.

The silver cup is still silver, as it is a cup. Therefore the supra-personal is fully personality and fully principle.

4

<u>CONSTELLATION</u>

Regard the Ultimate Principle
as a constellation –
a beautiful unity
of many beautiful stars,
sparks of light,
as pattern and glittering cloud,
light giving, overflowing in radiance.
Lights set in darkness,
Darkness illumed by light

5

TRANSCENDENTAL IMMANENCE

The Supreme Unity
expresses Itself as the multitude,
as one mind gives rise to myriad thoughts.
The transcendence of this Unity
rests in It's all-encompassing immanence

6

WATER

There is a well within each.
The water that is drawn
is humaneness.
When not obscured by impurities,
it is pure benevolence.
Life depends on it,
carrying the dead to new life.
Water from one source,
water as one source.
Water in all forms, in all places,
at all times
is still water
One Water,
myriad wells.

7

IMMANENT SOTERON

A goal for mortal life can be
to realise immanent grace-
acknowledging the sacredness
of the unity of all that is.
Holy is the All-encompassing Principle.
This can be called
the Immanent Soteron.

Inner Change

1
<u>THE GREAT DARKNESS</u>

The wholesome power of the universe rests in darkness.
Nascent patterns are strengthened.
Night supports seeds as a bed.
Universal power transforms into life. Bounteous beyond diminution is the universal power.
Black to charcoal are the shades.

Connected Meaning

Rest and contemplation are advised.
A clear mind with naturally address the issue.
Clarity uncovered presents.
Quiet reflection, but the answers will rise if themselves.
Go with what appears, having made discursive shaping.

2

HOUSE

Strong ascent of wholesome power.
Red is the colour.
A strong house is risen.
Food and learning.
Goat.

Connected Meaning
A change of focus is advised.
Engage the mind in another matter.
A full life embraces many things.

3

SEA

Wide sweeps the universal power. Expanding
horizons. Blue.
Sea journeys. Ships.
Balance in expansion.
Playfulness.

Connected Meaning
Active enjoyment inspires healthy discursive thinking

4

LUMINOSITY

Crystallisation and rest.
Beauty, rich and strong.
Upward, outward gazing.
Edification before great ascent. Attainment.
Luminosity.
Grasshopper.
Fly. Seal. Turtle.
The horns and the lamp.

Connected Meaning

Gratitude is good in itself, and edifies in effect.

5

AGRICULTURE

Strong, wide spreads universal power. Agriculture.
Purple. Metal.
Outwards.
Long land journey.
Enrichment. Harvest. Sweet.
Cat. Hen. Many animals.

Connected Meaning

Others' needs must be met. Others' well-being and emotion must be
contemplated and duly engaged with. Life provides the means. Take
effort to look for them.

6
CITY

Consolidation.
Inward looking. Remembrance.
Love.
Seeds awaken.
Compassion.
Red.
City. Lion.

Connected Meaning
Rest. Take note of dreams.

7
COLD

Strong power, stronger upward gazing. Great expansion.
Excitement.
Darkness and stars.
Black cat.
Cold.

Connected Meaning
Great excitement, a gamble. Trust to well considered action. Cleave to it. Great reward, or some loss.

8
PEN

Wide expansion of universal power.
A strong base.
Outward progress.
Blue and white.
Heart. Cake.
Pen.

Connected Meaning

Go with routine. Do little that involves great chance. Enjoy daily
life. Be content. Make effort to be content.

9
<u>DIFFICULTY</u>
Green.
A halt. Reversion.
Promise of great growth.
Divided. Difficulty. Anxiety.
Great potential.
Snow. Plant.
Home.

Connected Meaning
Consider with affection friends and family. Good fortune
approaches.

10
TWILIGHT

Marvellous culmination.
Blooms of great richness and beauty.
Wholesomeness. Great growth.
Twilight. Stars and moon.
Magenta.
Hammer and axe.
Revitalisation.

Connected Meaning
Gratitude to the Ultimate is always appropriate.
Gratitude for blessings may take effort.
Take stock. They are there.

11
DIAMOND

Great crystallisation.
Beauty and strength.
Diamond.
Approaching descent.
Yellow. Wind. Dolphin.

Connected Meaning
Limitations are in the way of mortal life. Take effort to reconcile
yourself with them, but do not be over anxious. All is as it should be
ultimately.

12
INTELLECTUAL GROWTH
Pain and rich beauty.
Purple.
Division.
Love and compassion.
Great intellectual growth.
Difficulty. Dog.
Sadness.

Connected Meaning
Sadness before new richness, progress, growth. Blessings and good fortune wait in store, though perhaps at a distance.

13
HEAVENLY POWER
Heavenly power ascendant.
Looking outwards.
Evening. Purple and navy.
Wolf. Starry vault.
Waxing strength.

Connected Meaning
Great experience. Blessed. Remember.

14

SUMMIT

Further culmination. A Summit.
Great heavenly power.
Beauty. Vital power waxing.
Lime green. Blue. Red.
Peak. Stars.
Closure.
Tiered descent viewed ahead.
Horse.

Connected Meaning

Great growth, experience. Exult, but accept limitation. Remember.
Consider and retain hope

Some thoughts, and the ghosts of thoughts.
'Evil seeds sprout evil flowers, bear evil fruit, return to sprout again.
If the vices of greed, joy in wrath, worship of human power lead to a death-dance
around atomic fire, the shame will be ours alone. The guilt will be ours, and the
working off of the great crime will be ours too.

If humanity devours itself, past that through a long age, summer will still be
summer, though no children to make play there. Earth will turn still until the
greater fire consumes it, the deepest black digests it, the darkness bring it's
memory home. Humanity has risen to dance at the ball, and over all now, death
holds greedy sway.
The Mind of Heaven habours countless thoughts and not all take human form.
Ceaseless are the turnings of Spirit in space, but the Mind of Heaven is eternally
still.

If we fail, we must take the test again: in another dreamtime, another turn in the
dark of space.'

Unity

Unity is the fundamental characteristic of existence. The universe is a unity. The person is experienced as a unity of parts, the Earth is a unity- a globe bearing life. Consciousness is a unity which unifies diverse perceptions through the senses across time. Unity, consciousness and existence are three aspects of the one reality. Unity precedes multiplicity. Multiplicity is unified in consciousness. Unity is at the root of all diversity. Break the unity of the living consciousness, body, the Earth-this is chaos and death.

In society, unity is expressed through solidarity, camaraderie, affection for the social environment, patriotism. In love between people, unity is the forgetting of an alienated self in the arms of the beloved. Love is profoundly unifying. Even desire is principle towards union.

In any project of politics, the virtue or malignance of the work and agenda depends on the proposed outcome, and the honesty of the enterprise. Beneficial political agenda must be based on a recognition of a society as a unity of people. A politics that seeks to affirm the unity of all the people must seek to bring them into mutual support, not competition, into mutual security, not violence, distrust or antagonism, must seek their shared prosperity and flourishing. Such a society would be characterised by harmony, which is unity in diversity. Such a society would be one where all citizens, no matter colour of skin, religious belief, gender or sexual nature, are assured a basic standard of living and the means and resources to fulfill their talents and live happy lives.

There is also a substratum to the unity of society: a unity of humanity and nature. Humanity has come from the elements and dynamics of the Earth. The Earth supports humanity's life. It is humanity's womb, it's table, it's house, it's tomb. Humanity and nature are not two, but one thing looked at differently. The Earth precedes humanity and contains it as a part of itself. To destroy, unbalance, exhaust the Earth is for the child to murder the mother while still in the womb

Unity is the characteristic of existence, and the preservation of life is in harmonious living. Harmonious living for a social animal is in beneficent political arrangement. Beneficent political arrangement must pay due respect to the environment in which the social animal has its life and support. Without such due recognition, any political agenda is academic speculation at best. At worst it's malignant apathy, desire for profit and power, and divisive, suicidal stupidity.

Sleep

'Deep in the ocean of darkness,
the spirit of the world sleeping sighs,
unending in cycle, rest then to rise
Soft stirring in silence
So rests this sighing world'

'And the Archangel guards
From out the navel's watch
Mystery pondering , he whispers in dream:

" *Rise not, sleep on, o world!*
no more again to pain.
your heavy days, though spying,
I sight, yet cannot reach
wake not, no more, o world.
wake never, not to rise"'

'But the world heeds he not,
Wheeling on a whirling breath,
to Dawn ever, to sleep
within the boundless, birthless womb
On Sacred waters sailing
in cycling, Sentient Night'

Lightning Source UK Ltd.
Milton Keynes UK
UKHW022004051222
413451UK00006B/130